confessions of a creative corporate clone...

written and illustrated
by robin hutchinson

dedicated to my dear husband-you are my rock,
mom, my role model, whom i love a "hole bunch",
my sisters and brother-you mean the world to me,
Kay-i think the world of,
the best in-laws and sister-in law,
friends near and far,
late fathers-e.g.r. and father john

this book is based on true stories that occurred when
i worked at a large corporation, which shall remain nameless.
no persons' names are mentioned, to protect the innocent.

anonymous survey...

we were given an online survey and told it was anonymous. we were also told that if we took the survey we would get a lolllipop.

in protest against, i chose not to take the survey.

the marketing department receptionist called me directly and asked why i hadn't taken the survey. anonymous?

cell phone hell...

while walking to the parking garage after work, it is fun to count how many people are on their cell phones.

they have just left their offices and walk outside to their cars speaking on their phones. really? what could be so urgent? "honey, i just left the office, walked outside to the parking garage and just closed the car door and...."

crash!! while pulling out, and talking on the phone, someone backed into someone else's casr.

almost every day i heard car crashes in the parking garage.

very important message..

the marketing director called a special meeting for our department to go through a deck (a deck is a stack of paper with information to give at a meeting) to discuss and explain why our department's name had changed.

thank goodness! i felt so relieved and i was able to sleep that night.

malaria madness...

during my lunch hour, sitting outside on a sunshiny day, i got bit by a mosquito.

i remember wishing i would get malaria so i could go home...

spending wisely

after laying off many employees, the company hired a dog trainer (for *beaucoup* bucks), to train the dog to chase away the geese that flocked around the corporate campus.

now, how do you operate this?...

we were, once again, in a meeting, and one of our guest speakers had a cd player to use for her presentation.

the director of marketing went to play the cd for the speaker and didn't know how to use it.

"now how do you operate this thing?"

the speaker came over to the player and started the cd. i'm so glad our director of a high technology company is so techno-savvy.

focus-shoot-aim...

the vice president of marketing wanted written instructions on how to use our department's digital camera so he could take his and his wife's pictures for their passports.

he would be needing them for his business trip to bermuda. poor soul.

you're joking...

our director wanted to liven up our monthly meetings. one co-worker jokingly suggested that at each meeting we take turns wearing a funny hat.

at the next meeting our director was wearing a joker's hat...

we all stared at each other in disbelief.

you shouldn't have...

our boss's boss invited us to his house for a christmas party.

we were asked to bring food and told he would provide the drinks.

how generous!

makes sense...

after laying off many employees, it was decided to redecorate the conference room with expensive chairs, tables and artwork.

makes sense, right?

no more treats

our department would celebrate each employee's birthday. the marketing director decided to stop the celebration of birthdays to cut costs.

no more treats...yes, those cupcakes, cakes and cookies are tremendously expensive.

hmmmm... cheesecake...

during a monthly meeting, a co-worker and i started discussing different flavors of cheesecake... one of our favorite places to eat is the cheesecake factory.

anyway...our supervisor gave us a disapproving look for not paying attention to the meeting. no sense of humor.

thank you for reading this book. hope you enjoyed it as much as i enjoyed did creating it.

if you have corporate stories you would like to share, email them to robin@artnology.us and they might be incorporated in the next book "*Corporate clones II*".

if you have a corporate job, try and be grateful for it. i know it's easier said than done, but when we find things to be grateful for in life, they multiply and it makes us much happier individuals.

as i look back on the corporate chapter in my life, i look at it with great appreciation. it provided financial stability, friendship, and some creativity.

if you are a creative soul, don't despair. there is light at the other end of the tunnel (and no, it's not another train). keep up the faith, keep creating and who knows? one day you may find yourself creating for a living.

these pages are for you to doodle on, make paper airplanes out of,
or write your own corporate story. happy creating!

the end